FOR THE GIFTS WE ALL COME BEARING

A Commonsense Approach to Relationship

© 2015 Jane A. Campbell, PhD

Sandy,
Thanks for the
gift of our friendship!

Jane Campbell

To the Five Guys, with love:
Pepe, Jose, Danny, Jimmy, and Joaquin
My great good teachers

ON BEING KIND
And this Book in a Nutshell

"Be kind whenever possible. It is always possible." —
Dalai Lama

The ideas in this book are perfectly ordinary. They are pedestrian, things you have seen quaintly cross-stitched on ancient samplers, in quaint museums. And that is the first point. Getting along with the people in your life—opening the gifts they come into your life bearing—is the simplest of matters. It is a set of clear choices, a very short list of rules you have probably heard repeated often. This book undertakes to put them all in one place, and to make the case, once and for all, that love is all you need.

Love may start out as the most elitist of all constructs. In your first experience of love, there is exactly one individual—your mommy, your daddy, a cute boy or girl down the street, or perhaps the family dog—whom you can't stop thinking about, whom you can't bear to be apart from, who causes you to harbor powerful emotions within your breast.

But the love, the loving-kindness, you need to minimize

friction in this peopled world is at the other end of a spectrum. The difference is like that between a laser beam and an incandescent bulb; loving-kindness has something in common with the candy heart a dunk in the river causes to melt inside Raggedy Ann. Loving-kindness is a *non*-elitist, democratic concept that has much more to do with how the other person feels than with how *you* feel.

The most important rule for acting on this kind of love involves taking care *of* the feelings of other people. We don't always care *about* the feelings of other people, but their feelings tend to impact us sooner or later. Said poet Maya Angelou, " I've learned that people will forget what you said, people will forget what you did, but people will never forget how you made them feel." If you think this is untrue or unimportant, then this book is not for you.

But if, on the other hand, you want know how to win friends and influence people (too bad for me Dale Carnegie wrote a book with that title in 1936), then you have come to the right place. If you are often rubbed the wrong way by people you know well, the recipe in this book is the recipe for you. If it is an ordeal for you to get what you need from the strangers you need to deal with—customer service representatives you encounter only over the phone, for instance—this book will help bring order to the process. If you feel there are walls between you and others, this book will help you understand where the walls come from, and what to start doing about them.

Maybe you know somebody like Bill[1]. Bill works with

his hands. On paper, he is a carpenter, but he does any kind of repair work. Bill can provide you with an education, but it's not an education you can get by asking him questions. If you want to learn from Bill, you can do it in two ways. You can watch him work—you'll start to learn how to fix things or how to build things. Or, you can study how he interacts with other people—you'll start to learn how to be the salt of the earth. Because if you give him half a chance, Bill will make you feel like a million bucks.

"How're *you* doin', babe" Bill will ask you, whether you are male or female. It's not a breezy, "How are you today?" that you might receive from a self-interested waitress or bag boy. It comes across as a real question, and it actually causes you to reflect on how you're getting by. Or, if someone or something has upset you, "Don't pay it no mind, now," Bill will say, in a deep voice turned to gravel by five decades of living. It's a soothing piece of advice, the kind that makes you feel that someone is in your corner, whatever you may face *out there*.

This talent of Bill's explains why his current employer quickly made him foreman when he was still a fresh hire ten years ago. Whether he knew it or not, the boss was well served by someone who could hear more than one side of an issue, who could connect on a feeling level with workers all over a job site. The workers themselves said they were comfortable with the way Bill treated them, and Bill's rapid promotion to foreman met with surprisingly little resentment.

None of this is to put Bill on a pedestal. Not all his

---

[1] Throughout, names and details are changed to protect identities.

decisions have been good decisions; not all his breaks have been lucky breaks. He doesn't have esoteric knowledge—he never went to college, he's never had psychotherapy, he would far rather watch football than read. He probably lucked into some aspects of his disposition, and he likely had the good fortune to see his gentle way of speaking modeled by someone in his past. Nevertheless, through good times and bad, he continues to choose to reach out in kindness to the people in his life.

♎

If the first point of this book is that getting along with people is the simplest of matters, then the second point is that doing so is a matter of choice.

We have already encountered the most important rule for getting along: accommodate the feelings of others. You might require more convincing of the importance of this idea; you might need to see a number of different examples to start recognizing the many situations in which kindness is really the main—or the only—issue. But you won't need to carry the idea into too many transactions to start to see how true it is that most of the time there is a choice. You can favor your own feelings, or you can favor the feelings of the other person. Every so often, there won't be a need to choose. But most of the time, there's a choice, and most of the time, the choice can go either way.

It's the same with the other rules on the list. You can choose to pay attention to them, or you can choose to ignore them. There are few enough of these rules that, by the end of the book, you won't really be able to object that you are confused, or that you can't remember them all.

You could argue, correctly, that they don't work every time. But you won't be able to argue that you have no choice.

The third point of this book is paradoxical. The third point is that getting along with other people—organizing your relationships well, becoming more open to the gift of relationship—may be simple, but it isn't exactly easy. It's not easy following rules when often, in the short run, you are rewarded for disregarding them. It's not easy to form new habits. It's not always easy to go slowly enough, to come up with a good response to a situation rather than tossing off a canned one. It is far from easy to be kind to someone who is abusing you. Knowing what to do—or at least what to try—is not the same as doing it with ease.

But on the other hand—and this brings us to the fourth point—in the long run it pays to take some trouble over the people in your life. It can be a lot of work, the rewards can look inconsequential—worse, kindness can often be mistaken for weakness—but the habit of kindheartedness can slowly but surely whittle away at the backlog of regrets many of us carry.

Alternatively, you can lie awake at night, fighting in your mind with other people, or maybe apologizing to them, or wishing in some way for a do-over; you can explain yourself endlessly to people who are not party to the interactions you are explaining; you can live with a reputation as someone who behaves inappropriately, abuses others verbally or otherwise, doesn't say what is meant, doesn't listen, doesn't care, doesn't tell the truth, and/or generally wastes the time of others.

Or, you can be kinder than that. You can be kinder,

wiser, more appropriate, more valuable, more a person of moral authority. You can get your relationships organized; you can strive to be, like Bill, the salt of the earth. Said psychologist Carl Jung, "I am not what happened to me, I am what I choose to become." Between the circumstances we find ourselves in and the decisions we make, it's the decisions that make all the difference.

ON BEING RECEPTIVE

"Courage is what it takes to stand up and speak; courage is also what it takes to sit down and listen." —British Prime Minister Winston Churchill

Each of us knows and feels more than we could ever express. That fact doesn't necessarily slow all of us down; some of us are on a hell-bent mission to express our every thought. Conversely—*per*versely—some of us are such acute listeners that we can stifle the most determined of chatterboxes. Somewhere in the ideal middle, a talker is talking, a listener is listening, and a relationship is moving forward.

Every once in a great while, someone comes along who is completely unaffected by his or her audience, but the great majority of us have a lot in common with sap-filled maple trees. Most of us are best able to bring forth what's inside by virtue of having someone willing to tap into it.

♎

Lawrence L. is a very senior professor at one of the most prestigious universities in the world. At first blush, Dr. L. doesn't seem like the ideal listener. If you happen to be his student, one of the first things you learn is that you only enter Dr. L.'s office on two occasions: when you have an appointment and when you are asking for an appointment. Formerly intrepid salespersons have been known to fairly run away from his office exclaiming quietly to themselves. (God only knows what possessed them to wander into Dr. L.'s office in the first place.)

Dr. L. is a certifiable genius; the President of the United States has awarded him the National Medal of Science. The President himself may well have been as nervous as any of Dr. L.'s students, or any hapless salesperson who misguidedly wandered into Dr. L.'s office. Dr. L. has been known to fall asleep while other professors are presenting their work. In short, to meet Dr. L. for the first time is *not* to find yourself thinking, "Well *here's* a friendly ear."

But two things give away Dr. L.'s great talent as a listener. One is that many of the colleagues of his long career, together with his over 100 doctoral students, count their relationships with him among the most important experiences of their careers. What these successful people have brought forth from inside themselves has often owed something, and in some cases everything, to Dr. L.'s willingness to lend them an ear.

The other thing that gives away Dr. L's skill as a listener is how seldom he is wrong. There is a story that dates back to his student days. Having listened carefully all semester to one of his math professors, and having received perfect grades on every assignment and test, one day late in the term, Lawrence (who was not yet Dr. L.) gave a ponderous reply to something the professor said in class.

"Not true," said Lawrence.

A horrified silence fell over the classroom—surely the professor was about to kick Lawrence out of class. Instead, the professor handed Lawrence a piece of chalk, and requested that he calculate a proof of the issue in dispute.

Shrugging in a manner his students would recognize half a century later, Lawrence moved to the chalkboard and began to write in a series of chicken scratches his far future students would also know anywhere.

The proof emerged slowly—quite a few lines of calculation were necessary. But by the end of about five minutes, the professor was nodding more and more decisively. Lawrence had indeed proved the professor wrong.

Make no mistake—a student who listened as well as Lawrence did was a gift to the professor, and the professor knew it.

The story of Dr. L.'s skill as a listener is a story about bootstrapping. The more he has listened, the more he's learned. And the more he's learned, the more he's learned how important it is to listen carefully. He certainly doesn't listen to everything and everybody all the time. He can't afford to. And by now, now that he has achieved the senior post at the prestigious university, his ear is exquisitely tuned to what is worth listening to and what isn't. A glance at his face is enough to tell you when you are wasting his time, and also enough to tell you when you are onto something.

Dr. L. throws one big party every year, at Christmas. His big house fills up with people grateful for the chances they've had to talk to Dr. L. throughout the year. Sooner or later, they've realized how lucky they are to know him. Fortunately for Dr. L., he also *knows* one or two good listeners. He is a student of good listening; he knows it when he comes across it. One professor Dr. L. never falls asleep on is one of these listeners, Dr. B. Said L., speaking of B., "Dr. B. paused before he spoke. He always does."

♎

One thing that might be going on when a listener pauses before speaking is that while listening, he or she hasn't been doing anything other than listening. He or she now needs at least a little time to think of what to say. But, said Stephen R. Covey, "Most people do not listen with the intent to understand; they listen with the intent to reply." We do this without realizing that we can't do both—we can't really pay attention to two things at once. But if we are listening with the intent of getting or staying on good terms with someone in our lives, we need to listen with this objective: to understand and remember what is being said.

This understanding may make us smarter in the long run. It may help us pass tests, get good grades, follow our boss' instructions, say clever things at cocktail parties. But when it comes to relationships, most of this is beside the point, if not actually counterproductive. Listening within a relationship isn't about becoming more knowledgeable in general, it's about becoming more knowledgeable about the other person.

When it comes to relationships, under the best circumstances, when you listen well to someone else, gifts are exchanged. As listener, you stand to gain whatever knowledge there is to be gained. The person speaking receives the gift of your listening ear. Over time, and with any luck, the two of you receive the gift of relationship. Any one conversation may be just one piece in a 1000-piece jigsaw puzzle--it's your choice what you do with the puzzle pieces. You can leave half of them in the box. You can put the puzzle together face down. Or you can put the puzzle together and enjoy in its entirety the picture created. It depends on how well you choose to listen.

ON KNOWING WHO'S WHO

"And Jesus spake unto them ' . . . render therefore unto Caesar the things which are Caesar's.' " —Matthew 22

Delphine is the heart and soul of charm and graciousness. Her greetings warm, her eyes sparkling with enjoyment or filled with understanding and compassion, she is a natural liaison, an ambassador of goodwill. She serves this function in her profession; she acts as a go-between for the law firm she works for and the government offices the firm has dealings with. But she also serves the same function at her church, in her neighborhood, at her children's schools, and almost any setting she finds herself in.

Delphine has an uncanny understanding of who's who, a grasp, at almost an architectural level, of who means what to whom. She knows the names of the bosses, of course, what their style is, what their background is, and how long they have been where they've been, but she also knows the names of janitors, secretaries, security guards. She knows things about people's children. Delphine likes nothing more than introducing people who have interests in common with one another, and matching up a person who needs help with another person who can provide the help they need.

Sometimes, Delphine simply wants the people around her to know about one another. This is the reason she one day told her neighbor, who was recovering from cancer, about another of their neighbors, who was recovering from a car accident. The next day, she told the car accident victim about the cancer survivor. Had Delphine simply delighted in sharing bad news, or were just in the habit of blurting out everything on her mind, she would have told the news to everyone and anyone. Her impulse was more helpful than that, though. Perhaps for the simple reason that misery loves company, both of her neighbors are glad of the information she gave them.

♎

General David Daniels is one of the youngest superintendents any of the military academies has ever had. He can be a man of steely-eyed determination but, a religious and old-fashioned man, he believes in loving-kindness. It is far more customary for him to have a twinkle in his eye.

Yet, said Aristotle, a friend to all is a friend to none. General Daniels finds himself making decisions that affect every being that lives, visits and/or works on a sprawling military base, every man, woman, child, quite a number of pet animals, two stables full of horses, and the occasional rattlesnake. General Daniels understands, uses, and enforces rank and protocol—a military establishment demands it—but another of his rules, spoken only on the rarest occasions, is that everybody is somebody.

General Daniels dates to a time before women were in the armed forces in any numbers, so his manners toward women tend to be courtly, but he applies his rule all around. Every woman is somebody, and he insists each one be treated respectfully. Every child, whether the child of a low-ranking enlistee or one of General Daniel's own children, represents the future, and every child is somebody. Every civilian is somebody. Everybody is somebody.

One day, General Daniels happened across the following scene near a facility on base: A woman in civilian clothing emerged from a car, which she had parked on some grass beside the road, and retrieved a toddler from a child-safety seat in the back seat. A major in uniform fairly barked at the woman, "You're going to have to move that vehicle!"

General Daniels, who was not in uniform and had gone unnoticed, intervened. An elderly man in the front seat of the car was also wearing civilian clothing. Gesturing toward the man and speaking in the calmest and softest of tones, General Daniels said, "Major, this man served in Normandy. He parks wherever he needs to."

♎

There are limits to how many people any of us can actually be in a relationship with. According to anthropologist Robin Dunbar, the number is somewhere around 150. In modern times, few if any of us live in isolated villages of 150, so in practical terms, Dunbar's number means people will come and people will go. Some will stick around, but more won't.

Rules like *everybody is somebody* give us powers beyond

Dunbar's number, though. Information-age tools like Facebook, Twitter, and the internet itself leave little excuse for remaining completely in the dark about who a person is, or for acting as if nobody is anybody. And why would you want to?

Minute by minute, each of us is building the world around us. Building a *better* world certainly isn't the undertaking of hasty, impatient people—it's easier to leave it as you find it. But in the fullness of time, kindness begets kindness. Listening to people well contributes to world peace. And, as Delphine and General Daniels begin to show us, knowing who people are—or remembering that no matter what they are *somebody*—gives us North Star-like guidance in how to treat them.

ON BEING TRANSPARENT

"Shut up and talk to me." —Singer/songwriter/recording artist Guy Clark

Isaac has been a professional mover for over three decades. Watch Isaac and another mover carry a heavy bureau down a flight of stairs—or more to the point, listen to them—and you are likely to hear far more from Isaac than from the other mover. "Ok, come to me," he'll say. "Hold up. I tell you what. We're gonna do this another way. Take it back up. You got your strap? I tell you what. Hand me my strap. Your strap too short. You got a grip? Get a grip, now. You don't got a grip you need to talk to me.

"Ok. Kick it. Lean it. You got it? Don't let it go, now. Ok, come to me."

Not every situation has the exact stakes involved in carrying furniture down flights of stairs, where, preferably, walls, stairs, furniture and humans all survive without a scratch. (The instruction to kick it is not a literal instruction.) But if each of us communicated as if staying out of a human/bureau avalanche depended on it, most of us would probably communicate better than we otherwise would.

Ian is a master seller. If you suspect he bases his entire livelihood on the craft of separating people from their paychecks, you are right. Ian says the only money doing anybody any good is money moving from hand to hand. He sells cars for a living—since some of them are used, he is the proverbial used-car salesman. Perhaps you find the idea laughable that Ian bases his entire craft on a willingness to be transparent. What used-car salesman was ever transparent?

But Ian's company gives him sales prizes year after year. He is a student of selling guru David Sandler. Said Sandler, "If you feel it, say it. Gently." Ian vowed long ago never to underestimate the people he sells to. In sophistication and opportunities to spend, American consumers are unlike anything the world has ever seen. Let them think for a second that you are withholding information from them, and they will find someone else to sell them what they want. But allow them to believe that their every transaction with you is an open book, and they will return to you time after time. They will send their friends.

There are certain personal questions Ian won't answer, his annual income topping the list. But as a matter of fact, his customers ask him surprisingly few questions. They tend to become preoccupied with *answering* questions, one of which might be, "I hope you won't take this the wrong way, but the economy being what it is, can you afford this?"

But to watch Ian fielding the questions he does get is to watch the master at work. He likes to lean back in his chair, feet up on the desk, a man with all the time in the world. He keeps owner's manuals, vehicle histories, copies of *Consumer Reports* and other magazines within reach, and will respond to technical questions with a patient thumbing through of whatever source might have the answer. Questions about the contractual paperwork are answered in a similar way, Ian moving a stubby finger below line after line of fine print until the exact language can be unearthed. Most customers wind up feeling they have less time than they thought for details. Their most urgent question tends to be about the colors available.

♎

Jacob is a complex and brilliant man, a man who perceives much more about the people around him than he ever puts into words. He's not reticent to speak, and you always know where you stand with Jacob. He just manages to get his point across with a well-practiced and refreshing economy of words.

Jacob's way of communicating dates back to two choices he consciously made while still quite young.

As a child, Jacob was bullied by his older sister Gilda. If their mother complimented Jacob, Gilda would use the next opportunity to tell him secretly that he was a mamma's boy. Very bright even as a child, he had the sense and imagination not to be a daredevil. Gilda would assure him he was a sissy.

Jacob had one moment of truth during his childhood the day he blurted to Gilda, "I'm a nice guy! I don't deserve you being mean to me!" Taking this stance didn't especially prevent his sister's meanness, but it made him feel good, and it was the beginning of his confidence in the spoken word. He was a child, and it would be years before he had words for what he was figuring out--words like directness, relevance, and succintness. But even a child can experience the power of words and the effectiveness of speaking one's mind.

As a teenager, Jacob had another moment of truth, this one about meanness. He noticed that it wasn't hard to fall into Gilda's same habit of put-downs. And how powerful words could be! Not only were words powerful, some of the time they were *too* powerful. Words could inflict an amazing sting! He knew this from watching what a rocky teenagehood his sister was having. She was suffering one falling-out after another over mean things she would blurt out to their schoolmates.

Meanwhile, Jacob enjoyed--thoroughly enjoyed--a wide circle of friends. Jacob vowed that although he always wanted to tell the truth, he would have a more guarded tongue than his sister. He never wanted to lose even one of his friends. In part it had to do with a respect for the power of words, a power he didn't want to abuse. Jacob grew fond of quoting Lord Acton, "Power tends to corrupt, and absolute power corrupts absolutely."

In effect, the two choices Jacob made about communicating balanced each other out. He determined that he would speak up about the most important things on his mind, but he also determined to have a tongue that was guarded against blurting mean things just because he could. He almost always thought before he spoke, and once he'd thought about some of the things he had the impulse to say, he often decided not to say anything. As an adult, Jacob has become a confirmed movie buff, a big fan of movie reviews. Some of the best movies dramatize the things he figured out about as a child about communicating with others. Jacob feels that movies capture the stories of life, and these stories are often about a search for what people most need to say to one another. He loves to read the best reviewers—they are onto the same thing.

A business owner, Jacob has a constant need to communicate clearly with his employees. He was well liked while still in school, and he is well liked today, including by his employees. But he nevertheless needs to maintain discipline, and trade being liked for being the boss from time to time.

An employee of his, Ricky, is a very good mechanic. One day, Ricky showed up drunk for work, and another worker reported this to Jacob. At this first instance, Jacob simply went to Ricky's workshop and asked him how he was doing. "Fine, boss," Ricky said, although their eyes met for a telling second.

A few days later, Ricky was drunk at work again. Jacob went to his workshop. "Ricky, here's what's going to happen," he said. "You were drunk the other day, and you're drunk today. You're going to go home, and I'm going to dock you your pay for the rest of the day. Take some time off, unpaid. If you still want to work for me in a few days, phone me."

A few days later, Ricky called, apologized for drinking on the job, and asked to keep his job. Jacob told him to be at work the next day.

The next day, Ricky showed up at 8:15, although starting

time was 8 a.m., and he was usually punctual. Ricky crept in the door, and sheepishly greeted Jacob. If he was expecting to give an explanation, he was surprised. "Ricky," said Jacob, "you can go to your shop and get to work on one condition." Ricky looked at Jacob expectantly. "I have no desire to know why you are 15 minutes late. Please get to work."

♎

Jordana was getting tired of calling her bank. Month after month, her statement showed a charge she shouldn't be receiving. Each month she called, and each month the charge was taken back off. But that didn't really solve the problem—Jordana didn't want to have to call her bank once a month to make sure she was being charged appropriate fees.

Jordana's fourth attempt to correct the situation went as follows:

"Thank you for calling Neighborly Bank. This is Lois speaking. How may I help you?"

"Hi Lois," said Jordana. "I'm afraid I am one of your," she paused. "One of your disappointed customers. That's not your fault, and it's not you I'm disappointed with. But I am disappointed. Do you think we could work together to solve my problem?"

Neighborly Bank had invested three weeks of paid training in Lois, and they had impressed on her that the bank wanted her to represent their trademark of "Neighborly."

"Well, I'm certainly going to try," she said. "What seems

to be the problem?"

"Ok. If you look at my latest statement, you will see I am being charged for going under the minimum. But if you look at my daily balances, you will see that I have never even come close to going under the minimum."

"Yes. I see that. Let me just remove that charge for you. One moment." And then, after a pause, "Is there anything else I can do for you today?"

Jordana caught her breath and then paused. She paused for such a long time that Lois eventually said, "Ma'am?"

With eyes closed, Jordana began again. "Lois?" she said. Jordana continued to manage not to *sound* angry.

"Yes ma'am?"

"Now remember, it's not you I'm upset with, but Lois, what would you need to do to make sure I don't get charged that charge again? That's what I need you to do." This time it was Lois who paused. "You do know that fees are how the bank makes its money, don't you ma'am?"

Lois was making the simple mistake of favoring her own feelings (or the feelings of her "team") over the feelings of her customer.

Jordana felt the blood drain from her face. Into the phone she said, "Hang on, Lois." She held the phone away from her ear. It was tempting to debate where banks made their money, but having paused, Jordana remembered where she stood (she was the customer), and rejected the bait.

She was drawing on a sense of who was who, as well as a determination to be clear.

Jordana imagined standing at the bathroom sink splashing cold water on her face. She gave her head a shake and put the phone back to her ear.

"Lois, here's the thing. Before you picked up, I heard a recording telling me that my call might be recorded or monitored for quality assurance. I'm guessing no one is monitoring this call right now; if they were, they would probably have broken in by now. Because they probably understand that no one wants to bank at a bank that makes them babysit the fee charges every month. So Lois, since no one *is* monitoring this call right now, I'm going to put it to you. Now remember, it's not you I'm angry with," (although this was beginning to be untrue). "But I am not happy. On the off chance that we *are* being recorded, I don't think you want to keep arguing with me. Do you think you could find someone who knows what to do so I don't need to get an unnecessary charge removed month after month?"

After a pause, Lois said, "Ok, ma'am. I'm going to put you on hold. It may take a couple of minutes, so please don't hang up."

After seven minutes, a different voice came on the line informing Jordana that she should not be seeing the incorrect charges ever again, and in fact she has not seen them again.

♎︎

It is hard to think of a more simplistic statement: if you

want to get along well with people, if you want your relationships to stay organized, communicate clearly. Well, no kidding. But judging by how badly much of the world gets along, each of the practices that go into having good relationships is strangely elusive. Being transparent, being timely, and keeping an eye on sincerity may be the most elusive.

As Ian, Jacob, and even Guy Clark have shown us, there are always more things to say than there is time to say them. As Jordana has shown us, there is much that tempts us to stray into long discussions, but long discussions are often much longer than they are informative. And anyway, being transparent isn't a simple matter of opening the floodgates and inundating somebody with information. If it were, we might think of the IRS with its voluminous tax codes, the local phone company with its multi-page bills, or the Encyclopedia Britannica as models of transparency.

Nor is the need for transparency a license to be unkind. If I think you are unattractive, unintelligent, or unworthy in some way, the less transparent I am about it, the kinder I am. And when the two trade off, as they sometimes do, kindness needs to trump transparency most of the time.

Transparency is like kindness in being a matter of communicating intentionally. Kindness involves communicating, through words, deeds, or what *isn't* said or done, the same simple idea again and again—"I mean you no harm," or "I come in peace," or even, "I wish you well."

But transparency involves communicating *novel* information or knowledge of some sort; it changes constantly depending on what is needed. It can be something concrete and objective—the day and time of a party you are throwing. Or it can be something quite subjective—just how you're feeling, or what you are or are not willing to do. Perhaps you are unwilling to listen to a lengthy explanation, or get into an irrelevant discussion.

Very often, at any given time, there are a small number of things, or even a single thing, a single piece of information, that a relationship needs—truly needs—to be conveyed. Figuring out what that exact information is is well worth the search.

ON BEING TIMELY

"Seize the day." —Roman poet Quintus Horatius Flaccus (Horace, 65 BC – 8 BC)

The passage of time is the most inevitable of natural disasters. Good looks fade, dust settles into things, parking meters run out. Even if we did confine ourselves to a roster of 150 relationships, chances are there still wouldn't be enough time for enjoying each one. When we are children, every wait seems endless; for better or worse, it feels as if we have all the time in the world. But in reality, whoever coined the phrase "all the time in the world" was quite the optimist.

We can approach this inevitability pessimistically, or we can rise gamely to the challenge. Because when viewed correctly, life is one long series of fleeting opportunities.

♎

Tina's story helps illustrate the challenges of being timely. She started life as an expert on what happens when no one is timely, and became an expert on what timeliness can buy.

Tina grew up in a chaotic household. Once, when she was quite young, a forgotten saucepan caught fire on the stove—it was Tina who raised the alarm. One time, having been given the wrong date, guests showed up a week early for a party. There was also the time when Tina was eating dinner with her family, and a friend and the friend's mother appeared at the door, ready to pick her up for a forgotten sleepover.

Tina's parents approached life with a kind of bumbling gusto. Their household was characterized by forgetfulness and distractibility, but the truth was, Tina's family was also generous, fun loving, creative, and more. Tina's parents strove to impart to their children the belief that people were to be valued—the more the merrier.

Tina wanted to honor that belief but, more introverted than the rest of her family, she found it excruciating to think others saw her as bumbling. School was her salvation. At school she began to catch on to the rewards available to people who could keep their things, their papers, and their commitments in some kind of order. By the time she was in her twenties, she was reading everything she could get her hands on about time management and efficiency; it led to the career she began in her thirties as a professional organizer.

One of the things Tina eventually read was an article claiming that people could be clutter. It went against everything she had been brought up to believe, and in her head, she argued silently with the author for several days after reading it. The article recommended "breaking up" with high-maintenance friends or friends who carried mostly negative energy. Upon re-reading the speeches the article suggested for accomplishing this, Tina realized she could never bring herself to do something that seemed so rude.

She knew there was a grain of truth in what the author was saying, though. Life was too short to spend it on the *non*-enjoyment of people. So Tina determined that she would take a glass-half-full approach to the whole issue, and strive to fill her life with as many pleasant interactions with people as she could comfortably fit in.

There were opportunities everywhere she looked. And without going so far as "breaking up" with people, Tina determined that she would learn to bow out of situations that made her *un*comfortable--or that needlessly consumed precious time. With the help of a therapist she happened to be seeing, she was learning to actually value her introversion, to value other people anyway, and to protect herself from social overwhelm.

Thanks to her profession—for instance, she is a follower of productivity guru David Allen—Tina is a careful user of a planner/calendar and an avid maker of lists and notations. Thanks also to her profession, she has mastered something her parents never conquered: competent time management. Tina has put at least one clock in every room in the apartment she and her family share, including her walk-in closet, and has conditioned herself to check the time religiously.

Tina has no natural sense of time, but she has developed a profound respect for how important time is. Accordingly, one of the first things she teaches her organizing clients is so-called time management (called this though time will never cease to manage us). Tina makes her living by helping busy, ambitious householders get out from under the clutter in their lives—combining all her many interests, she strives to reduce household chaos one family at a time. It is no accident that her work takes her into households that remind her of the one she grew up in.

When Tina first shows up, what's at the top of the typical client's mind is how quickly the clutter can vanish from specific places in the home. But Tina only works with clients who are ready to start thinking differently about their management style. Having a client who isn't ready to listen to Tina is the kind of uncomfortable situation she has learned to bow out of. The first question she strives to teach her clients to answer is, "When?"

Sometimes, she'll work with a client who repeatedly lets phone calls interrupt their sessions. Typically, the client hasn't made much progress in Tina's absence, and they are squandering the opportunity now.

When she has worked with the client for a few sessions, if the client's phone rings, Tina goes out on a limb. She grabs the phone, and as it continues to ring, she looks at the caller id and tells the client who's calling. "Knowing I'm still on the clock, are you sure you have time to speak to this person *right now*?" The call almost always goes to voicemail.

Often, Tina will have a client who is a woman who does a lot of picking up after other family members. Tina asks if anyone is teaching the children to pick up after themselves. "If they aren't learning it at home," she'll ask, "when will they learn it?"

One of her clients is a woman with a huge office containing exactly one chair. The woman is running a household with two children, and also running a home-based business whose principal is her husband. "When do you feel most overwhelmed?" Tina asked her.

"When I'm in my office."

"When do you get in touch with the many things you need to discuss with your husband?" Tina asked her.

"When I'm in my office."

"When does it hit you how badly you need your children to pick up some slack around the house?"

"When I'm in my office."

"When are you and the family best able to sit down and talk?"

"When we're at a restaurant."

"I'll tell you something the restaurant has that your office doesn't."

"Pasta pomodoro?"

"Chairs."

"Oh, but I can always pull chairs in from downstairs . . . "

"How often do you do that?"

"Twice since we've moved in."

"Exactly."

"You think I should put chairs in my office?"

"Are you getting enough teamwork from your family now?"

"No, but we *like* eating out!"

"It's an opportunity to enjoy one another's company. All the more reason you shouldn't use the occasion to discuss who does the laundry! You need to move that discussion to a different 'when.' "

Another of Tina's clients is near and dear to her heart because she reminds Tina so much of herself. Tiffany is happy-go-lucky and good-natured—she can be running twenty minutes late and act like she has all of that proverbial time in the world. Tiffany avoids confrontation like the plague; she would much rather daydream; she would much rather deflect tension with humor or a change of subject.

For some time Tina had been striving to help Tiffany improve her system for making a to-do list. "I don't see the point of writing lists and lists and lists," Tiffany kept saying.

"Forgetting what you wanted to do must not be that big a problem for you," Tina finally said one day.

"Are you kidding?? I'm constantly forgetting what I wanted to do. Until it's too late, of course."

"I wonder why you resist planning, then," said Tina. Tiffany shook her head and shrugged.

"Name something you've been wanting to do," Tina suggested.

"My nails," Tiffany said with a laugh.

"Ok. Good one."

"Do I really have to put "do my nails" on a list?"

"Maybe not. But you do need to do your nails at a time when it won't cause you to be 20 minutes late to something more important. You do need to have your time management well enough in hand that you have the wiggle room to do a manicure within a day or so of needing a manicure. Name something else you've been wanting to do."

"Give roses to my boyfriend."

"Oh that's a *very* good one! What has been stopping you from giving roses to your boyfriend?"

"Ironically enough, I wish I was bringing him roses when I'm on my way to see him and I'm running late. But stopping for roses would only make me later! And it *really* disappoints him when I'm running late."

"What does he say?"

"He says he's respectful of my time, and he wishes I could do the same for him."

"How do you feel about that?"

"It's only a few minutes."

"How many is a few, and how often are you late?"

Tiffany's eyes teared up at this.

Tina waited while Tiffany composed herself. Then she said, "Would you like to give him roses even if you weren't running late?"

"Yes, absolutely! It's just that I only think of it when I'm running late!"

Tina responded, "There's no one right way to plan your time, but can you see how it might be worth a lot if you could plan not only to give your boyfriend roses but to be on time for him too?"

Yet sometimes it isn't teaching Tina is after so much as simply showing consideration for her clients' busy schedules. During an economic downturn, in a time when many businesses still dealt with paper checks, Tina realized that quite a few of her clients were business owners and would respond well if she offered the service of taking their checks to the bank and making deposits more quickly than they could. She was exactly right. Said one of these clients, "That is the nicest thing anyone I've ever hired has ever offered to do for me!" The client has remained loyal ever since.

♎

Tina is like Lawrence L. in that both display competencies in spite of themselves. Both have made the conscious choice to excel at their respective competencies. Dr. L. has mastered listening despite the fact that he sometimes willingly refuses to listen. And despite a near complete dependence on the external trappings of time—clocks and timers and so forth--Tina has chosen to master time as much as anyone ever does. The lives of both are filled with people who are grateful to know them.

Few things speak more loudly about how we feel about other people than the way we treat their time. And we will only ever have a finite number of chances to enjoy our children while they are still children, enjoy our ancestors while they are still alive, and get and stay on good terms with the people who are important to us. Given that there aren't enough hours in the day to spend with the people who matter to us, it is all the more important to make every minute of a relationship count.

ON WISING UP
And Keeping It Real

"... not to utter words, but to live by them." —John F. Kennedy

Watch enough really good acting and you come to realize that, at least temporarily, it is possible to produce an almost perfect facsimile of something you are not. With enough rehearsals or outtakes or desperation, you can create realities out of falsehoods. Do this in real life, and the proverbial tangled web quickly results—what people believe about you takes on a life of its own. Wrote Kurt Vonnegut, "We are what we seem to be."

This cuts many different ways. What it means on the bright side is that what you wish were true can become true. As the saying goes, if you want a friend, be a friend. Seem to be a friend, actually become a friend. Some of the time, it works.

But it also means you can't believe everything you'd like to believe. True, the rules for getting along with others can be boiled down to a simple few. But that fact notwithstanding, and though we are what we seem to be, we are still complex. Any assumption we make about anyone will need to be revisited, possibly revisited many times.

There is something beyond kindness, beyond receptivity, beyond knowing who's who, beyond transparency and, although intermingled with the passage of time, even beyond the passage of time. Call it sincerity--it has to do with whether, today, you or the people you know are telling the truth with things said and unsaid. Sincerity also has to do with wavelength--the mutual ability of two people to truly be attuned to one another. It is a separate dimension, and it bears keeping separate tabs on.

I may act like a friend, wish at first to be a friend, and even seem in my own mind to be being a friend--or, as the case may be, an honest business person, or an ethical politician, or sincerely whatever else I claim to be. Alternatively, I can seem at first *not* to care, even though I do. But however much we consciously try to seem like what we want to be, there are deep and unconscious things inside all of us, and they will leak out. They will show up in our facial expressions, our body language, a tremor in our voices, the things we leave unsaid, the questions we leave unanswered, the ways we close a door, the doors we leave closed once we've closed them, the chairs we do or do not set out for others, and so on and so on.

We are wise to be mindful of cues like these from other people, because such cues can help us keep an eye on our assumptions. Cynical though it may sound, we have an instinct to look beyond whether someone *acts* happy to see us, for example, or *seems* to believe strongly in what they are saying, and it's a good instinct.

It bears remembering that others are applying the same instinct to us. They will look beyond our smiles and the words we utter; they are likely to see patterns we ourselves are unaware of. It's important to stay wise to others, and to know whether they are being true to *themselves*. Just as importantly, though, with a little mindfulness, others can be wiser to us than we are to ourselves. This is one of the gifts they can bring us--they can discourage us from self-deception, and help us stay true to *ourselves*.

As if this weren't complex enough already, who we are can and will change. But in spite of all this, it is within our grasp to be our best selves--at our best, who we are consciously trying to be is in alignment with who we deeply, unconsciously, and sincerely are.

♎

A four-year-old boy stands to one side of a room with his finger in his nose. From the other side of the room, his grandfather tells him to take his finger out of his nose. The finger stays where it is. The grandfather repeats himself. "Take your finger out of your nose." The finger stays put.

The grandfather begins to stride across the room. Before he has taken a third step, the boy has whisked his finger away from his nose.

What we say and what we really intend can travel in such different circles that a child of four knows to test for the difference. Because it is rude to conspicuously challenge the sincerity of others, we tend to grow out of it. It is a useful instinct to keep up our sleeves, however.

Ω

If you have ever caught yourself weeping at movie, or maybe a beer commercial, you have gone to the opposite extreme from the four-year-old boy. Whereas he has tested the sincerity of someone who is equipped to pass the test--whereas he has *advertised* his disbelief--we can find ourselves *suspending* disbelief, and perceiving real sincerity when we *know* it has been manufactured. Perhaps we take pride in our softer, more sentimental sides; also, we seem to want to believe in others. We seem willing to give the benefit of a doubt that isn't even there.

We make assumptions as part and parcel to thinking; to think is to make assumptions. We seem to assume at least some of the time that others are well-meaning. We are okay with being moved by a beer commercial, as if assured that buried in it somewhere are good intentions. And perhaps it is healthier to err on the side of general goodwill. Being kind, accommodating the feelings of others, is more important than any other aspect of getting along with others, and this is easier the more we believe in the loving-kindness of others.

But where unreality can really begin to set in is in our tendency to deny in ourselves, and overlook in others, feelings that are less beautiful although just as real--if not more so. Our feelings are our feelings; sometimes each of us is hostile, or fearful, or sad, or self-seeking, or competitive, or a combination, or a shade on any of these and other dimensions. Maybe we humans do act partly out of goodwill, but on the other hand, some people do outright lie. And far more than putting us in touch with our better natures, the point of a beer commercial is selling beer.

Not everyone who brings tears to your eyes is a friend. The cute boy or girl from down the street, say--or the beer company--may not be in any kind of a relationship with you at all. And this is the main question to be answered when looking at the sincerity of a person you know. Everybody is sincere about some things and some people. But what is their relationship *to you*? Is it as you first assumed it was; is it what you wish it was?

♎

The six competencies of relationship--kindness, receptivity, perceptiveness (about who's who), transparency, timeliness, and wisdom (about sincerity)-- can tend to strain in opposite directions from each other. We have already seen that we can't really listen and inform at the same time; that's just one example. Contemplating the elusive concept of sincerity can bring home the point that better organizing your relationships may be simple, but it isn't entirely easy.

If you were in a relationship with Bill from the chapter on kindness, for instance, what would the relationship look like? Bill sincerely cares about the feelings of others, and much of the time, having our feelings accommodated by a friend is all we ask. But as we learned from General Daniels in the chapter on knowing who's who (and also from Aristotle), a friend to all is a friend to none. If Bill were to see you being *unkind* to someone else, or even a nearby dog, it would suddenly no longer be your feelings he cared about--he cares about kindness in general. How much he liked you would depend on how kind he thought you were. And when it came to knowing what was unique about *you*, or listening to you rather than watching the next football game, you might eventually realize that Bill wasn't the closest friend you'd ever had.

It is very pleasant to know Bill. If you *were* to watch a football game with him, he would go out of his way to make sure you were happy and comfortable. Bill might not be all that receptive, perceptive, or transparent, but he is kind. Most of us would be wise to be more like Freddy a lot of the time. But kindness is not always sufficient on its own. The best relationships entail a tuning in to what we think and who we are, in addition to how we feel; our closest friends insist that we face facts, even when they are uncomfortable facts.

Alternatively, if you knew Dr. L., from the chapter on being receptive, you would probably forego being treated with absolute kindness from time to time. Dr. L. isn't looking to be unkind, but as an educator, he sees it as his responsibility to discourage the talking of nonsense--he cares deeply about telling the truth.

Despite the occasional unkind glance, however, in the long run, if you were permitted to have a relationship with Dr. L. (unlike the misguided salespeople), Dr. L. would listen to you carefully, and it would be a relationship that was sincerely about you in all your uniqueness. If someone listens to you well, you can't be sure their reaction will be positive, but it will sincerely be about you. Dr. L. is not a friend to all, and like his students and those fortunate enough to receive Dr. L.'s collegiality, you would probably be grateful to be among those he did befriend.

The need to know who's who can also strain against

sincerity, even for someone as genuinely gracious as Delphine. It can be hard to reconcile sincerity, mutual co-existence on a wavelength, with caring about who's who the way Delphine does. Without meaning to or even realizing it, she can place high expectations on the people she knows. She likes them to fit together nicely; she likes them to get along well together. Having two people she knows and cares about have a falling-out is deeply disappointing to Delphine.

But most of us would also be wise to be more like Delphine a lot of the time. *Not* knowing who's who is a good way to be slightly out of it much of the time. Nevertheless, it can be a little hard to manage the less-than-beautiful, perhaps non-conformist, parts of who you sincerely are around someone like Delphine. If you knew her you might have to choose: pretend to like someone more than you do, or live with disappointing Delphine. Both Aristotle (a friend to all is a friend to none), and Dunbar the anthropologist (with his 150-person limit) might be paraphrased as saying that our abilities to be on the same wavelength as other people are distinctly finite. Delphine is no exception.

Many of us would also be wise to be more transparent a lot of the time. But not for nothing do we have the cliche, "Don't shoot the messenger." We have already seen that being transparent can strain against being kind. It can strain against remaining tuned in as well.

Information changes us. It isn't easy to warmly embrace someone who is telling you something you don't want to hear, certainly not in the short run. If you are the bearer of the information, you may well have your motivations and sincerity questioned, at least in the short run.

Someone who combines transparency with staying on good terms with people has typically learned to walk a fine line to keep information from coming between them and other people.

If you knew Ian the master seller, for instance, and thought really carefully about what he does with information and what it means about the sincerity of the relationship you have with him, you might end up wanting to follow in his footsteps and go into sales. Ian may ask you questions a friend would ask--whether you can afford to buy a car right now, for instance. But Ian's aim isn't winning your friendship. Much of what he is doing is less about *you* than it may seem. His aim is selling cars to you and the people you know.

Accordingly, he gives you every scrap of information you ask for. But he isn't terribly likely to volunteer extraneous information. He has learned that emulating the Encyclopedia Britannica doesn't make him more likable. Also, he has learned that telling people things they already know can insult them. So unless he thinks it will get him sued, he will go so far as to withold information no one has asked for.

One other thing we can learn from Ian is the way he strives to be transparent *and* kind. Bear in mind how he phrased his question about money: *"I hope you won't take this the wrong way,* but the economy being what it is, can you afford this?"* He has learned to consider the emotional impact exchanging information can have, and does what he can to acknowledge and accommodate feelings.

Ian walks the fine line between transparency and staying

attuned by curbing his transparency occasionally--
withholding a little bit of information from time to time.
In the case of the chronically unpunctual Tiffany, on the
other hand, her *lack* of transparency is straining against
sincerity, which is paradoxical, since she is not a
deliberate withholder of information. Although ideally
she will become more punctual, in the meantime, in the
age of the cell phone, she could take *some* stress off her
relationship with her boyfriend if she took the time to let
him know as soon as she got behind schedule.

Although Tiffany is an extreme case, most of us would
also be wise to show greater respect for the time of the
people we know, and to think more about our timing in
general. Time is priceless; even the longest life is too
short for squandering its minutes and years. Nevertheless,
being timely can strain against sincerity. No one likes a
clock-watcher. Staying ever-mindful of scheduling is
likely to win you admonitions to relax. So-called time
management is like religion and politics--there are limits
to how much one can talk about it in polite society. In
terms of staying sincerely attuned with others, staying on
schedule is a thing best tended to behind closed curtains.

♎

Sincerity would seem to have something about it that is
like the tide. Tending to the other competencies--and
also, simply staying generally open to the unpredictable
things the knowing of people can bring--both of these can
cut us off from these very people, at least temporarily.
But over time, and with the best relationships, the effort
pays off; the connections flow back.

You could try to keep all the sometimes contradictory
competencies in mind at once, trying to be kind *and*

receptive *and* perceptive *and* transparent *and* timely *and* wise. But if you did, getting along with the people in your life—opening the gifts they come into your life bearing—could suddenly start to look like quite a daunting task, neither simple *nor* easy. Each of the competencies will serve you, just not all at once. Fortunately, with any given person, improving on the relationship will likely be a matter of focusing on a single one of the competencies--being kinder, perhaps, or being more transparent. Attunement over time with even a single other human being can make it all worthwhile.

GIFTS

"Blessed are they who have the gift of making friends, for it is one of God's best gifts. It involves many things, but above all, the power of going out of one's self, and appreciating whatever is noble and loving in another."
--Author Thomas Hughes

It has been said that the ideal gift is something the recipient desires, but not something he or she would have given himself or herself. Nowhere is this description more fitting than in the gifts people come into our lives bearing.

Sometimes, particularly in times of stress, we actually use other people. Using other people has nothing to do with the giving or receiving of gifts.

At other times, we ask things of other people; often, we expect things. There's nothing wrong with asking or expecting. After all, owning one's needs and desires and speaking up for oneself is part of being transparent, and being transparent is one of the critical relationship competencies. But asking and expecting cause the giving to be ever so slightly less than priceless. The gift *of* relationship, and the gifts that come *from* relationship--the best of them--only come through biding one's time, and through getting and keeping one's relationship habits in good repair.

♎

Gladys is a registered nurse and Ann is her patient. There is something self-effacing about Gladys. Her posture is slightly hunched; she carries her shoulders too close to her ears. Her smiles and laughter seem a bit forced.

Having been in the intensive care unit for over two days, Ann is becoming overwhelmed by the steady parade of different nurses. Nevertheless, looking at Gladys' name tag, she asks one of her standard ice-breaking questions. "Gladys, where are you from originally?"

Much of Gladys' life story emerges in the time it takes her to check Ann's vitals and empty Ann's surgical drains. She's originally from the Bronx. She was married to the wrong guy, who fathered her three children before leaving them high and dry. Gladys moved back in with her mother, went to nursing school at night, and over the course of 10 years, strung together the requirements for ICU work through an unconventional series of internships and jobs. She married another man, who was a sweetheart, but he died too young. Other ICU nurses have often challenged Gladys' path to ICU work, but, says Gladys, for once forgetting to force a smile, "My dues have been paid."

Overwhelmed, and preoccupied with the trade-offs between pain and pain medications, Ann does little more than punctuate this story with automatic prompts: "I'm sorry to hear that," "What happened then?" and the occasional, "Wow!" Hearing about Gladys' treatment by the other nurses does catch her attention. Still, her only comment about them is, "They didn't approve, hm?"

But Ann is in the habit of kindheartedness; perhaps it is this that has Gladys opening up in the first place.

Gladys is on duty the next day, when Ann will be moved to the regular ward. Gladys tends to Ann's needs, and they chat matter-of-factly about how Ann's night went and what the weather is doing. As Gladys pushes Ann's bed down the hall, she tells her, "The nurses here will take very good care of you. I'll be staying back in the ICU." It's as she's locking the bed into place in Ann's new room that, with an *un*forced smile this time, she gives Ann an unexpected gift. "But I just want to thank you for being a beautiful patient!"

Ann has lain in a bed doing very little for Gladys other than following her story, lending a friendly ear. She tries to smile back, but somehow Gladys' thanks have moved Ann to tears.

♎

George had everything he could ever need, and in fact boasted that, although he expected to live another 20 years, he would never again need to go clothes shopping. The only problem was that his three grown children longed to give him gifts.

George's friend Wilson picked up on the frustration of George's kids.

"George," said Wilson. "You need to let your kids give you something."

"Whatever for?" said George. "Don't they know I have everything I need?"

"What you need is to let your children feel needed. Haven't you ever shopped for something and *not* found it?"

"Ok," said George, after giving it some serious thought. "I wanted a stuffed toy aardvark. One of them could get me a stuffed toy aardvark."

"Correction," said Wilson, whom George had corrected many times over their long friendship. "You clearly need *three* stuffed toy aardvarks."

George asked for a gift that he *would* in fact have given himself, and by the time the three distinctly different stuffed toy aardvarks arrived, they were hardly an unexpected gift. In this case, however, it was George's three children who received a priceless gift: knowing what gift would please their father.

♎

As we have seen, Jacob's sister Gilda alienated many people as a youngster. Thanks in part to Jacob's good influence, she eventually wised up, and sought out professional help with anger management.

There was one friend in particular, Maya, whom she had always regretted losing. To her amazement, through

Facebook she received the remarkable gift of a second chance with Maya. One day Maya commented on a post by a mutual acquaintance, and Gilda realized that she could reach out to Maya with the simple tapping of a few keys.

Not having seen Maya in years, Gilda reflected daily for almost a month about what she wanted to do with this tremendous electronic power. What would she say? What did she wish would take place? What was the worst that could happen?

Finally, she drafted a message. She thought about showing it to her anger management counselor, but she realized that if the counselor advised her against sending it, she wasn't sure she could comply.

"Hi Maya," she wrote. "I just want you to know that I have come a long way since high school.

"People who are close to each other tease each other. People we knew in those days teased each other, and I envied the way they seemed close enough to do that.

"I was completely off-base, though, and I really had no idea how to gently tease a person. All I knew how to do was abuse people. For whatever it's worth, I somehow magically thought the things I said to you were a part of our closeness. The fact is that for all the criticisms I heaped on you, I earnestly wished I could be more like you.

"If I could eat the words I was always hurting you with in those days, I want you to know that I would." And since she had made up her mind not to ask for a reply, and to simply settle for sending the message, she ended with, "I don't know what else to say. Over and out. Gilda."

She sent the message, and tried to be done with it. But for a day and a half she had to fight an almost hourly urge to check for a reply. She had decided that the worst that could happen would be complete silence from Maya, but she realized she hadn't worked out just how long she would wait before giving up hope.

"Hi Gilda," came the reply at last. "Please put your mind at ease. It's good to hear from you. Maya."

♎

Most of the time, the gifts brought to you by other people are small and subtle things. A thank you, a chance to present someone with a trifle, acceptance of an apology or, alternatively, a smile, a joke, an interesting or useful piece of information, and so forth--at their grandest, these are not earth-shattering matters.

At their best, they seem inconsequential. At their worst, they can look like something you would go out of your way to avoid. Take the unkind glance Dr. L. might give you if he caught you talking through your hat. Or take any piece of information you found disappointing or inconvenient. Only in hindsight--if at all--would you be likely to recognize these things as gifts you'd been given.

Anyone anywhere can give you one of these gifts, however, whether a disguised gift or otherwise. Your own openness to the possibility can be a multiplier.

♎

At any given time, you are connected to a cloud of something like Dunbar's number of people-- approximately 150. Some of them are passing through the cloud once and once only. Some of them may be in your cloud for the rest of your life. Some of them may stick around for a while but depart eventually. Some of them may depart and come back at a later time.

You probably don't have the power to make it much more than 150. If you are famous or especially powerful, you might be able to touch the lives of more people. But if you are connected to a lot more than 150 people, convincing them, or letting all of them convince you, that what you have is an actual relationship with them all--this will probably take powers neither you nor they have.

But you do have enormous power. Over time, you have the power to organize the 150 such that most of the time you are interacting pleasantly with people who don't get on your nerves. You have the power to become more open to the many gifts, however small or subtle, the many someones around you can bring. You have the power to give gifts of your own which, however you intend it, will encourage the giving. The mosaic you are able to put together in this way may contain the occasional piece of unpleasantness. But in the main, approaching others with loving-kindness will tend to fill your life with a pleasantness that quickly overwhelms and distracts you from the unpleasant.

You have the power to be kind to almost everyone you encounter. This keeps things more pleasant in and of itself, and it also tends to keep your options open. Hardly ever does anyone need to know how eager you are to have them enter, or leave, your cloud of 150, or to stay out of it altogether.

You have the power to lend a friendly ear whenever you want to and think you can afford to. Almost all of us *dis*organize our relationships through failing to listen quite well enough. Beginning to listen with the single-minded purpose of understanding and remembering what is being said by the important people in our lives can be an immediate way to get on better terms with them.

You have the power to pay more attention to who's who. Any business person who lives by the art of networking will encourage this as an almost foolproof way to get ahead--any of the relationship competencies will serve efforts to get ahead. But attending to who's who for the naked purpose of getting ahead will strain against doing it for the purer reason of simply being more open to the gift of relationship.

Some of us tend toward the cryptic and could stand to be more transparent, whereas others of us could stand to be slightly less transparent, or at least to temper our transparency with more kindness. But in both cases, we have the power, and in fact the right, to say what is on our minds. Transparency may be the competency with which we do the most to take care of ourselves; taking responsibility for our own needs, wants, and intentions helps in the long run to keep us on better terms with others.

You have the power to be more timely. Taking steps to do so, for instance by always being the first to leave, may get you some flak, but being a seizer of opportunities will gradually begin to surprise and delight the people around you.

Lastly, you have the power to wise up. Our thinking about the sincerity of others can tend to be slightly wishful. In the main it's probably accurate to believe that most people mean well most of the time. Still, it can be important to look beyond what words people utter and how they consciously act.

By the same token, it's very important to know that others will do the same to you. We can put enormous effort-- throwing parties, buying flowers--into trying to *seem*. The safest thing to do is to strive always to *seem* as you truly *are*. Abraham Lincoln is supposed to have put this nicely, "You can fool some of the people all of the time, and all of the people some of the time, but you cannot fool all of the people all of the time."

It's also hard to improve on the way Shakespeare put it. "To thine own self be true, and it must follow, as the night the day, thou canst not then be false to any man."

This is not to minimize the importance of seeming; it is worth working at. If you want to be open to others, you will want to seem that way. It is a light you will want to let shine.

♎

Up close, a mosaic looks like a lot of colorful chips surrounded by cement. It's impossible to tell, from up close, whether it's a good mosaic--one depicting something interesting and beautiful, with subtleties of color, shade, and light--or a bad mosaic. What you need to make that call is to step back and gain perspective.

Anyone who comes into your life can bear you a gift. Sometimes, the *person* is the gift, and what you get is the gift of an entire relationship. But relationship or not, the unlikeliest people can give you the nicest things when you least expect it.

Create a good mosaic with the people in your life, and with perspective, you will begin to see something more interesting and beautiful.

ACKNOWLEDGMENT

Eternal thanks to Michael Van Kleeck, long suspected of not even being mortal.

Made in the USA
Charleston, SC
10 April 2015